Overcoming Acne

Overcoming
Acne The How and Why of Healthy Skin Care

Alvin, Virginia,
and Robert Silverstein

Preface by Dr. Christopher M. Papa

Illustrated by Frank Schwarz

Morrow Junior Books   New York

Text copyright © 1990 by Alvin, Virginia, and Robert Silverstein
Illustrations copyright © 1990 by William Morrow and Company, Inc.
Preface copyright © 1990 by Dr. Christopher M. Papa

Printed in the United States of America.

1 2 3 4 5 6 7 8 9 10
Library of Congress Cataloging-in-Publication Data
Silverstein, Alvin
    Overcoming acne : the how & why of healthy skin care / by
Alvin, Virginia, and Robert Silverstein ; illustrations by Frank
Schwarz ; preface by Dr. Christopher M. Papa.
        p.   cm.
    Includes index.
    Summary: Describes how pimples form, discusses the causes
of acne, self-treatments, and when to see a doctor, and outlines
strategies to limit or prevent acne.
    ISBN 0-688-08344-7
    1. Acne—Juvenile literature.   2. Skin—Care and hygiene—
Juvenile literature. [1. Acne.   2. Skin—Care and hygiene.]
I. Silverstein, Virginia.   II. Silverstein, Robert A.
III. Schwarz, Frank, ill.   IV. Title.
RL131.S55   1990
616.5′3—dc20   89-13748   CIP   AC

Acknowledgments

The authors would like to thank Dr. Christopher Papa, Clinical Professor of Dermatology at the UMDNJ–Robert Wood Johnson Medical School, for his many insightful comments and suggestions for this book. In the many years that he has treated various family members, we have been continually impressed by his expertise, and by his compassion and understanding.

Thanks, too, to our astute and capable editor, Andrea Curley, for her encouragement and helpful suggestions.

Contents

Preface

Oh, is there not one maiden here,
Whose homely face and bad complexion,
Have caused all hopes to disappear
Of ever winning man's affection?

The naive hero of *The Pirates of Penzance* clumsily proposes to a bevy of beauties, and W. S. Gilbert exploits a comic situation which survives the test of time. This popular playwright typically dealt with human fears and foibles by poking fun at them. Acne, the obligate badge of adolescence, is a painful, universal experience. The condition not only wreaks havoc in the difficult teens, preying on the sensitivities of the uncertain changelings, but continues to intrude throughout the adult years.

Fortunately, there are strategies which can limit or prevent acne, and, failing that, new medicines to bring reliable relief. Being armed with sensible information is the first step in the war against acne. With knowledge of the common contributory factors, an understanding of what *not* to do, and appropriate self-treatment, most acne can be curbed. If not, professional assistance from an appropriate physician will be rewarding.

I first met the authors while treating a family member who had acne. The first visit lasted more than a half hour. There is always a reason for the eruptions, and we had to find out what it was. What kinds of lesions were present? What was their exact location? Were they related to specific activities at home, school, or play? Was time of month or diet important? Methodically, each avenue of inquiry focused on the specific personal events of the particular patient. Each is different with special individual problems and special solutions. When drugs were prescribed, the reason and mode of action were explained. The patient was shown how to use the medication and told what to expect, both in benefits and potential side effects. If a physician is unwilling to spend the time to seriously treat acne, search for another.

Proof of the authors' confidence in the educational approach is reflected in this book. Readers who put the advice into practice will usually see their needs met, and many will avoid trips to doctors. The few who require a physician will be in a better position to evaluate the quality of the professional assistance, and actively participate in the joint effort to achieve healthy, clear skin.

Christopher M. Papa, M.D.
University of Medicine & Dentistry of New Jersey
Robert Wood Johnson Medical School
New Brunswick

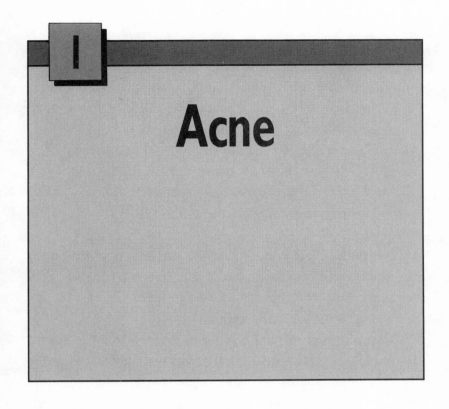

Acne

Tonight is the big night. You've been looking forward to the school dance all week. Now it's almost time to go. You glance in the mirror while you're washing your face. Oh, no. . . . What's that on the tip of your nose? It's big and awful. It's a zit! "Why *me?*" you cry.

If you have that common skin disorder called *acne*, you're not alone. Close to 90 percent of all teenagers are bothered by acne sometime between the ages of twelve and seventeen. For some it's only an occasional pimple or so. But for others it could mean painful red sores all over the face, neck, chest, and back. Most people grow out of acne by their late teens, but for some it can last until their twenties, thirties, and forties. Acne can also leave behind scars that cause psychological stress for a person's whole life.

Most people don't think of acne as a disease or a disorder. It's just one of those awful things teenagers have to face while growing up, and there's really nothing much you can do about it.

Not so!

Why people get acne is still partly a mystery and, like the common cold, acne has no cure. But skin specialists and researchers know enough about acne so that almost every case is treatable.

Although doctors are not sure exactly why it starts, they have a pretty good idea of how it develops. After all, they've had a long time to study acne. This condition has been around for as long as there have been people—teenagers have been plagued by acne for thousands of years.

King Tut, the best-known Egyptian pharaoh, was only in his teens when he died. Scientists can tell that this famous teenager had the same problems with pimples as teens do today. Various medications were put in Tutankhamen's tomb to help treat his acne problem in the afterlife.

Everyone knows what the blotches, blackheads, and pimples of acne look like, but there are many myths and misconceptions about this condition. Lots of people have lots of different ideas about what causes acne and how to get rid of it.

Generally, when we think of acne we think of *acne vulgaris.* (*Vulgaris* in Latin means "common.") It is a disorder of the hair follicles and their attached oil glands in the skin, and its symptoms can vary from just a few pimples to many deep cysts.

WHY TEENS?

Most people get acne during adolescence. It seems unfair that this extra burden should be added, just when a boy or girl has so many other upsetting adjustments to cope with. But the acne process seems to be linked with the whole sweeping complex of changes that occur in the adolescent body.

During the teen years the body is flooded with hormones that stimulate many changes. *Hormones* are chemicals that help to control and coordinate body processes. Different hormones are produced to regulate nearly everything that goes on inside us. Growth hormones stimulate growth, for example, and sex hormones control sexual development. Adolescence is a time when both these types are produced in abundance.

At puberty the pituitary gland, the master gland that is found at the base of the brain, tells the body to start making sex hormones. In boys the main sex hormone that is produced is testosterone, which is made in the testes. In girls estrogen and progesterone are produced in the ovaries. Testosterone and progesterone are chemically very similar, and together with the estrogens, they belong to a class of compounds called *steroids*.

In addition to sparking a rapid growth and development of the sex organs, the sex hormones stimulate the formation of secondary sex characteristics, such as breasts in a woman and facial hair in a man. They also cause the oil glands in the skin to grow larger and secrete more oil. Sometimes, though, too much oil is produced. This may result in acne.

Most adolescents eventually outgrow acne. That is, it usually goes away by itself. But it may be years before it stays away. During that time, many teenagers often feel uncomfortable about their "spotty" complexions. They may feel awkward about the way they look and tend to shy away from people and activities because of their self-consciousness. Worse yet, in severe cases scars can remain behind to haunt a person for the rest of his or her life. Many people will try anything to get rid of their acne problems.

Unfortunately, there is no miracle cure for acne. No injection will cause pimples to disappear overnight and stay away. You can't take a pill to banish unsightly spots. Controlling acne is something that has to be worked on every day, and treatments do not produce immediate results. Often it takes one to two months of treatment before an acne problem is finally under control. Even then you have to continue the treatment, or else the pimples may come back.

You may be able to keep an acne problem under control by yourself. Nearly 90 percent of all people with acne don't go to a doctor. Instead, they try to deal with their acne by using one of the countless products available from supermarkets and drugstores. However, if you decide your acne is too much for you to handle on your own, you may wish to see your family doctor or a skin specialist, called a *dermatologist,* for help.

Even with a dermatologist, the battle against acne is a team effort. You will have to follow your doctor's recommendations carefully every day.

Whether you fight acne with a doctor's help or on your own, you should know as much as possible about it so that you can understand what's going on in your body and how you can best help conquer those annoying spots. This book will help you by describing how pimples form and what today's medical specialists know about the causes of acne. In later chapters you'll find out how to treat pimples on your own, when you need to see a specialist, and what a dermatologist can do to help. But first let's find out more about the part of the body that acne affects most directly—the skin.

2

Our Remarkable Skin

Beauty may or may not be only skin deep, but the skin is the part of us that other people see. Inside, we may all have the same basic assortment of organs, but it is our outer appearance that makes us look unique. Even the skin on our fingers carries a set of fingerprints that no one else has.

The skin reveals a lot about our inner selves. It grows pale when we're afraid and flushes when we're excited or embarrassed. It always gives us away when we're tired. Doctors can be alerted to possible internal diseases, such as diabetes and liver disease, just by examining the skin.

THE WALL AROUND US

The skin is a protective shield around the body, keeping out harmful things such as bacteria and pollution. It's naturally waterproof and will not allow water past its protective shield even when submerged for long periods of time. Skin helps to give the body shape and form and keeps important fluids and our internal organs inside and safe from harm. It protects the body from heat and cold by regulating the body temperature. Unlike a coat made of cloth, which no longer fits when you outgrow it, the skin can contract and expand like a balloon. Think of all the times you ate just a little too much, and the skin on your belly s t r e t c h e d, only to return later to its normal size. The skin grows around us as we grow taller and wider. It also has an amazing ability to repair itself if it is cut, torn, or burned.

Our skin is more than just a self-repairing, protective overcoat, though. It is an organ of the body, and a very active one, at that. It helps to rid the body of excess fluids, salts, and wastes. Some skin cells are like miniature factories, producing a variety of hormones and other substances and carrying out various chemical reactions. (Under the action of sunlight on the skin, for example, vitamin D is converted to an active form that helps to control the formation of bone.) The skin is also a sense organ that brings us information about the world: Through it we feel pain and pleasure, heat and cold.

It may seem a bit strange to think of the skin as an organ, like the heart or brain. What is even more surprising is that it is the largest organ in the body. If all of a person's skin were stretched out, it would be large enough to cover a tabletop or a door—twenty square feet or so—and it weighs about eight pounds. The skin is made up of billions of cells, each microscopic in size. These cells are constantly being replaced. A skin cell lasts less than a month from the time it is formed until it falls off and becomes a tiny flake of dust. That means that every month you have a completely new skin covering on your body.

The skin is divided into three basic layers: the epidermis, the dermis, and the subcutaneous layer.

THE OUTER LAYER

Did you know that every skin cell that you can see is dead? No, you're not suffering from some mysterious disease. This is a perfectly normal state of affairs for the amazing outer covering of your body. The outermost layer of the skin is called the *epidermis.* (*Epi-* means "over"; it lies over the *dermis,* the layer that makes up the bulk of the skin.) The epidermis is about as thick as a sheet of paper. It is composed of fifteen to twenty layers of cells stacked on top of each other.

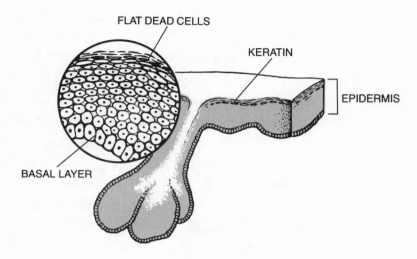

Epidermis

New cells are created in the deepest part of the epidermis, called the *basal* layer. Cells reproduce by dividing. As the skin cells get older they are pushed upward toward the outer surface of the epidermis by new cells that are forming. As they move outward, they become flatter, accumulate a horny protein called *keratin,* and start to lose precious moisture that keeps them alive. Eventually, by the time the epidermal cells reach the outer surface, they are completely flat and have lost most of the cell fluid. The nucleus—the "brain" that holds the instructions for all the living cell's activities— has disappeared.

It takes an epidermal cell about two weeks to reach the upper layer on the outer surface of the body. This layer is exposed to the air, which would quickly dry and kill living cells. But the cells of this outermost layer are all dead, and they form a hardened protective shell called the *stratum corneum* (literally, the "horny layer") over the living cells beneath. At some time during the next two weeks the dead cell falls off or is washed away—perhaps speeded in its departure by the rub of a towel or the scratch of a fingernail. The loss of dead cells from the outer layer of the skin is a natural process that goes on continually. Normally we don't notice it. But when dead skin cells are shed too quickly, psoriasis or dandruff may be the result.

The epidermis serves mostly as protection for the body. In addition to providing a physical shield, this part of the skin also protects us from the damaging ultraviolet rays of the sun. The basal layer of the epidermis contains *melanocytes,* cells that give the skin its color by producing tiny particles of the pigment *melanin.* Melanin particles absorb the sun's harmful ultraviolet radiation and keep it from damaging the body's delicate cells and chemicals.

A fascinating thing about melanocytes is that everyone has basically the same number of them. The reason there are people of many different colors in the world is that each person inherits genes that tell the melanocytes just how much melanin to produce and how big each melanin particle will be.

When skin is exposed to the sun, the melanocytes produce more melanin. This extra pigment produces a darkening effect—a suntan—and provides better protection. People who are very fair may not be able to make enough melanin to protect themselves effectively. Then the ultraviolet in the sun's rays can damage skin cells, producing a painful sunburn.

THE LIVING SKIN

Beneath the epidermis is another major skin layer, the *dermis*. Its name comes from the Greek word for skin, and this layer makes up about 90 percent of the skin. All of the cells in the dermis are alive, and they are

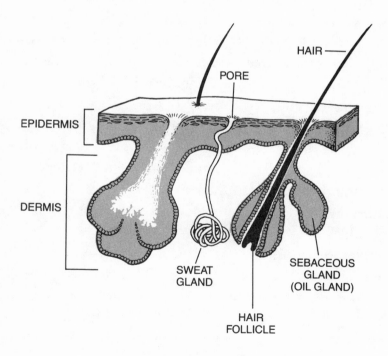

Dermis

nourished by a rich network of millions of tiny blood vessels, called capillaries. The dermis also contains numerous nerve endings, as well as hair follicles, sweat glands, and oil glands. They are all held in place by a strong yet very elastic substance called *collagen,* which has been called "nature's nylon."

If harmful microbes get into the dermis—perhaps through a cut or scrape in the protective barrier of the epidermis—they may begin to multiply, producing an infection. Then another series of body defenses goes into action. Chemicals released by the damaged cells cause the walls of the tiny blood vessels in the skin to get leaky, and fluid from the blood seeps out into the tissues. This process is called *inflammation.* Disease-fighting white blood cells squeeze their way out of the capillaries and roam through the dermis on search-and-destroy missions against the invading microbes.

The dermis gives the skin its strength, yet can stretch to allow the body to move freely. (As we age, the dermis grows thinner, and the accumulated effects of the years and exposure to the sun make it lose its elastic springiness; gradually it stretches out and sags, producing wrinkles.)

This important skin layer also contains a number of sensory nerves that end in specialized sense receptors. Some respond to heat, others to cold. Some are sensitive to the slightest touch, some to a firmer pressure; still others provide warning signals of pain when skin cells are being damaged.

The network of tiny blood vessels crisscrossing the dermis brings oxygen and nutrients to keep the epidermal cells alive and carries away their waste products. The capillaries also expand and contract to help cool the body down or warm it up. When the air around you is hot, special sensors in the skin send messages along nerves to the brain. These messages spark a new set of signals, which cause the capillaries to expand. Then they have a larger surface for radiating heat, which passes out through the skin directly to the air or is taken up by the water in sweat, which carries heat out of the body. Cold air against the skin surface is also reported by skin sensors, prompting signals that cause the capillaries to contract. That decreases their radiating surface and helps to conserve body heat that would otherwise be lost through the skin. The body's system of internal "thermostats" fine-tunes the various processes of conserving and releasing heat, so that the inner body temperature stays at about the same level no matter how hot or cold it is outside.

When the capillaries in the dermis expand, the reflections of the red blood cells that they carry give the skin a rosy color. (Not only heat but also emotions can spark this reaction. That is what happens when you blush in embarrassment.) When the capillaries contract, they take up a smaller fraction of the skin area, so not as much of the red color is visible. Then the skin turns pale. (This reaction, too, can be produced by strong emotions.)

The tiny coiled tubes of the sweat glands are found

in the dermis but extend up through the epidermis and end at the surface in openings called *pores*. Sweat pores are too small to see with the naked eye. Over the entire body surface, there are betwen two and five million of these sweat glands!

SWEAT: WHO NEEDS IT?

Some people sweat more than others, but everybody sweats. The major functions of sweating are to remove unwanted waste products from the body and to help regulate the body's temperature. Sweating goes on whether you visit the North Pole or bask in the sun on a tropical island. Heat produced by the muscles and by various chemical reactions in the body is taken up by the watery sweat and carried out to the surface of the skin, then discharged into the air when the water evaporates. When it is hotter and the body heat builds up faster, you sweat more. Sometimes so much sweat is produced that it forms visible drops that roll down your face or soak your shirt. (A baseball pitcher working on a hot summer day may sweat out more than a gallon of fluid in a single game.) When it is colder you sweat less, although some sweat is still being formed. Even when you cannot see or feel any wetness on your skin, about three cups of sweat evaporate from your body each day.

There are two types of sweat glands. The most abundant are the *eccrine glands,* the sweat glands mainly involved in the body's temperature-control system. They produce a thin, watery sweat containing water, salts, and a body waste product called *urea*. The ones in the palms of the hands and the soles of the feet are particularly sensitive to emotions. When you are about to give a speech or bat in a tight ball game or meet someone who is important to you, you are likely to find your palms sweaty. The *apocrine glands,* the other type, are found only in the armpits, genital area, and nipples and typically empty into hair follicles. The secretion of apocrine sweat glands is a sticky white, gray, or yellowish fluid containing a number of complicated chemicals. This kind of sweat is a part of a communicating system that humans do not use very much (at least, not consciously) but many of our animal relatives depend on: communication by scent messages. Each person (or animal) has a characteristic "odor signature," produced by chemicals in the breath and various body secretions. This odor may vary, depending on a person's physical condition or emotional state as well as various body cycles. Animals use scent to mark off their home territories and to announce to other members of their species that they are ready to mate. Scientists are not sure yet how much of a role scent plays in human life, but they do know that the sweat from the apocrine glands is the main component of "body odor."

The apocrine glands do not become active until puberty. So, although young children sweat, their perspiration doesn't have the "smelly" odor typical of adults. Actually, it is not the sweat itself that smells. The odor results from the action of bacteria that grow on the sweat. Apocrine sweat is smellier than eccrine sweat because it contains much larger amounts of organic chemicals (good bacteria food). Body hairs also help to trap moisture close to the skin and provide more surfaces for bacteria to grow on—and the places where apocrine sweat glands are found are usually rather hairy. Bacteria grow and multiply faster in hot temperatures, which is why your underarms are smellier in the summer than in the winter.

In addition to cooling the body and getting rid of wastes, sweat helps to lubricate the skin cells on the outer epidermis and keeps them from being worn away

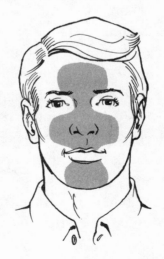

Areas of sebaceous (oil) glands

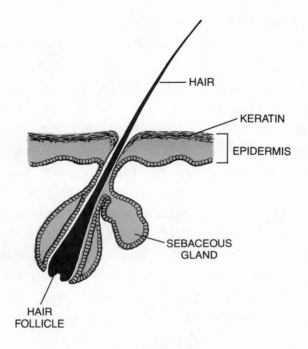

Sebaceous gland

too quickly. The skin is also lubricated by another type of gland found in the dermis, the oil, or *sebaceous,* glands. Sebaceous glands are found in the skin of many parts of the body, but they are concentrated mostly on the face, neck, upper chest, and back. In some areas of the face there are about two thousand oil glands per square inch! There aren't any oil glands on your lips, the palms of your hands, or the soles of your feet— areas that are completely hairless. (But anyone who has ever had sweaty palms or sweaty feet knows there are plenty of sweat glands there.)

THE NATURAL OILS

Sebaceous glands secrete their oily substance, called *sebum,* into tubelike *hair follicles* that extend up through the epidermis and open to the surface in pores that sometimes are big enough to be seen without a magnifier. They are particularly obvious in places like your nose and forehead. (The nose is not usually hairy, but each pore contains a tiny hair that may not grow long enough to reach the surface. Sebum tends to build up more in these pores than in those with longer, thicker hairs.)

The inside walls of the follicle are lined with epidermal cells, even though they extend down into the dermis. Imagine sticking your finger into a balloon. The rubber wall of the balloon snugly covers your finger and lines the tubelike hollow it produced. Like the epidermal cells on the surface of the skin, the cells lining the follicle are constantly being replaced, and the older ones are shed. However, since they can't fall off into the air like those on the surface, they fall off into the follicle. Sebum carries these dead cells out of the follicle and onto the skin. When the follicle contains a hair, the follicle wall wraps tightly around the hair, and the oil oozes around the hair shaft and out to the surface.

Sebum plays some important roles in keeping the skin healthy. It cleans out dead cells that are shed from the follicle lining and also flushes out bacteria that grow in the follicles. It grooms the hair, keeping it from getting brittle and giving it a healthy shine. Sebum also helps to lubricate the skin, by trapping moisture that keeps it soft and smooth. In addition, sebum creates a slightly acidic coating on the skin that keeps away harmful bacteria.

The epidermis—the part of the skin that we see—and the dermis, which contains the roots of the hairs and a

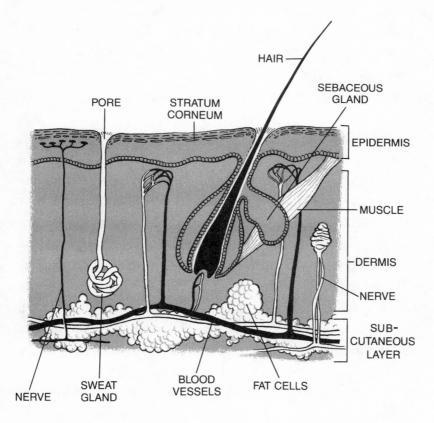

Epidermis, dermis, and subcutaneous layers

variety of glands and sense receptors, might together be thought of as the skin proper. They rest on the innermost layer, a nourishing and supporting structure called the *subcutaneous layer*. Here, a sturdy framework of connective tissue is interlaced with arteries and veins and contains fat cells. This layer serves to insulate and protect the muscles, bones, and internal organs. The fat deposits serve simultaneously as heat shields, shock-absorbing cushions, and emergency energy reserves for times when food is scarce. The subcutaneous layer is more developed in women, giving them more protection and softer-feeling skin.

YOUR MICROBE MENAGERIE

You may be rather surprised to learn that your skin is covered with bacteria—billions of them! A single square centimeter of skin in your armpit or on your scalp may teem with a million of these tiny microbes, although the same skin area on your forehead might support only two hundred thousand or so, and a square centimeter of skin on your forearm might be populated by a mere ten thousand bacteria. These are just the numbers on the surface; perhaps ten times as many bacteria live in sheltered crevices, inside the hair follicles. The skin's bacteria come in a variety of forms. Some are rod-shaped bacilli; there are also cocci that look like tiny round balls. The particular bacterial population may vary from one person to another. It may also vary on different parts of the body.

Normally this *microflora* lives quietly on the skin, sheltering among the outer epidermal cells, basking in the warmth the body provides, and feeding on bits of dead cells and waste products. No matter how thoroughly you washed, you would not be able to get rid of more than a small fraction of these bacteria, but that is actually a good thing. The normal skin bacteria help to protect us from invasion by harmful disease germs by producing antibioticlike substances that keep other microbes in check. If they get out of their normal habitat, though, and penetrate into the bloodstream, some of these normally helpful bacteria can run wild and produce harmful effects. In fact, one common form of skin bacteria contributes to the problems of acne.

Acne starts in the middle or dermal layer of the skin. During puberty the sebaceous glands, like the apocrine glands, are stimulated by hormones to produce more secretions. However, the adolescent body may produce more oil than the skin really needs. It accumulates on the skin and hair, giving them a shiny look and a greasy feel. More cells are sloughed off in the follicles, because of the larger amounts of oil passing through. Bacteria thrive on the rich food supply. Gradually the increased amounts of oil, dead cells, and bacteria accumulate. Sometimes they clump together and stick to the follicle wall, eventually forming a plug that is the beginning of the acne process.

3

The Life of a Pimple

Pimples usually seem to pop up overnight. This may sometimes be the case, but more often the pimple that you notice has taken weeks, even months to develop before you ever see it. Once it does appear, it might disappear in a day or two, or it could linger on for another few weeks or even months.

There are many different kinds of acne pimples, or *lesions,* as doctors call them. They can take the form of tiny skin-colored bumps, little white bumps, small red bumps, bigger red bumps, bumps with a black substance in them, pus-filled bumps, or even giant, painful ones. All of these are acne lesions, and all of them start out the same way: from a follicle that becomes blocked.

HOW PIMPLES START

When shed epidermal cells start clumping together, along with the oily secretions and bacteria feeding on them, they begin to stick to the follicle wall. As more cells pile up, the wall grows thicker and it becomes more difficult for sebum to flow to the surface through the narrowed channel. The tube-shaped follicle starts to bulge a little as more and more shed cells stick to the growing mass inside it, and the opening to the surface becomes increasingly blocked. At this point, the problem is still a small one; you would need a microscope to see the plugged-up follicle.

Doctors call any stopped-up follicle a *comedo* (plural *comedones*), and a tiny microscopic one is called a *microcomedo*. All acne pimples start out as microcomedones. Unfortunately, they don't stay invisible. Eventually, thousands of dead epidermal cells build up in the follicle, and the plug makes the opening to the surface even smaller as it grows. The plug is not solid; it is more like a sponge. The skin cells in it are loosely clumped together, allowing oxygen and some amount of fluids to go in and out.

Meanwhile, the follicle starts to really bulge like a tiny balloon under the skin, because the sebaceous gland keeps producing sebum. Some of the sebum gets out to the surface, but most of it is trapped inside. Now the

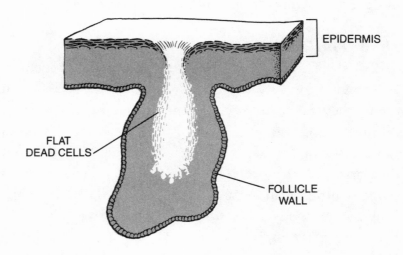

Microcomedo

comedo is big enough to see if you look at yourself in the mirror. When pimples are first visible, they appear as tiny white or flesh-colored bumps under the skin. They may be hard to see, but, if you stretch or pull your skin they become more evident. Because they are almost completely plugged, these acne lesions are called *closed comedones*. They are also known as whiteheads. Dermatologists sometimes call them "time bombs" because they may not seem like much—they are only about 2 millimeters across, roughly the size of a pinhead—but they can develop into very serious kinds of pimples.

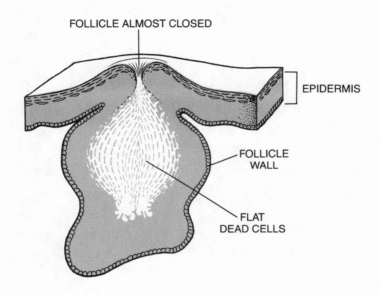

Closed comedo

It is important to remember that the opening of the pore at the surface of the skin is not where the block occurs. It is down inside the follicle, so simple washing cannot clean the plug away. Often skin will grow over the pore, preventing almost all sebum from escaping and making the pore opening almost impossible to see.

THE BLACKHEAD STAGE

Oil and dead cells continue to build up, and eventually one of two things will happen. Either the sebum will eventually force its way out to the surface of the skin,

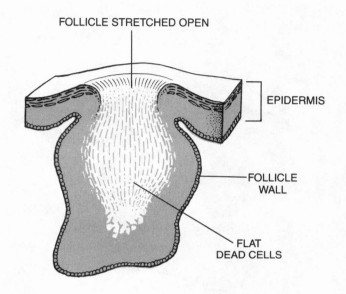

FOLLICLE STRETCHED OPEN

EPIDERMIS

FOLLICLE WALL

FLAT DEAD CELLS

Open comedo

or it will put so much pressure on the follicle walls that they burst like a balloon that has too much air in it. If the pore eventually does open, it produces what is known as a blackhead or, in dermatological terms, an *open comedo*. People call it a blackhead because there is a gooey dark material inside.

The biggest misconception about blackheads is that the dark stuff is dirt and it is caused by not keeping the skin properly cleaned. The dark color is actually produced by a chemical reaction of the sebum and dead cells with the oxygen of the air. The skin's own melanin also makes a substantial contribution to the blackhead's dark color. In fact, since melanin is produced only by the epidermal cells in the upper part of the follicle and not by those lining its lower part, the material in the open comedo is dark near the skin surface and lighter below. The color of blackheads also varies from one person to another, depending on the amount of melanin in the skin. Dark-skinned people tend to have very dark blackheads, while albinos have white ones. Since the matter in the comedo isn't dirt, more frequent washing will not get rid of it. Neither will squeezing: Although some of the material near the surface will be forced out, the narrowing of the follicle down below still remains, and the blackhead will eventually re-form.

FROM BAD TO WORSE

Annoying as blackheads may be, the alternative can be worse. The second outcome of a closed comedo—an exploded follicle wall—is a much more serious situation. For the first time, the acne process enters the body. (Remember, the follicle wall is really an extension of the outer layer of the epidermis, so in a way open comedones and even closed ones do not occur "inside" the body.) When the follicle wall is damaged, the dead cells and sebum flood into the dermis, along with some of the bacteria that were living in the follicle. This is when inflammation starts, and with it come redness and swelling.

Now the body's defenses spring into action. When tissues are damaged, they send out chemical distress signals. A substance called *histamine* makes the microscopic capillaries dilate (widen), bringing more blood into the area. One side effect of this is that the capillary walls become leaky, and fluid from the blood oozes out into the surrounding tissues, producing swelling and inflammation. The chemical distress signals sent out by damaged tissues also summon white blood cells, which act as combination soldiers and garbage collectors. They are the body's main line of defense against things that do not belong in it. Some of the white blood cells slip through tiny gaps in the capillary walls and move into the damaged tissues, prowling along the fluid-filled spaces between cells.

Soon the inflamed pimple is the scene of a fierce battle. White cells, looking like constantly changing blobs, creep through the tissues, homing in on bacteria, dead skin cells, or bits of sebum. The white blood cells flow over their prey, literally eating them. (The technical name of these germ-fighting white cells is *phagocytes,* which means "eating cells.") The battle rages on as the white blood cells tirelessly gobble down bacteria and bits of dead matter. Some of these blood-cell soldiers are overcome in the fight, "slain" by doses of poison produced by the bacteria they have consumed. These dead blood cells, along with dead bacteria, sebum, and bits of skin-cell debris, accumulate in the form of the whitish matter called *pus.*

In the first stages of the battle, the increased flow of blood to the region of the damaged follicle makes the swollen area look red. Soon it becomes noticeable at

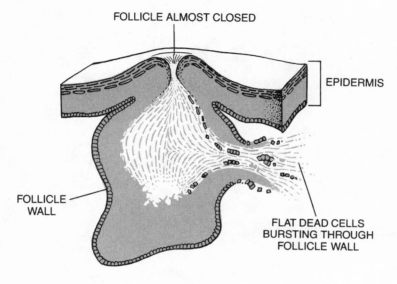

FOLLICLE ALMOST CLOSED

EPIDERMIS

FOLLICLE WALL

FLAT DEAD CELLS
BURSTING THROUGH
FOLLICLE WALL

Papule

the surface of the skin, in the form of a small red bump called a *papule*.

If there was only a small break in the follicle wall, the white blood cells will quickly win the fight and remove all the intruders within just a few days. The papule will disappear, and the follicle wall will be patched up with scar tissues. Sometimes the papules become hardened and remain for weeks before their contents are finally absorbed.

Often the damage is more extensive and cannot be contained right away. As the fight continues, a sac of pus forms, filled with oil and bacteria and white blood cells. At the surface, it looks like a yellowish or whitish cap on top of the red bump. It has now become a

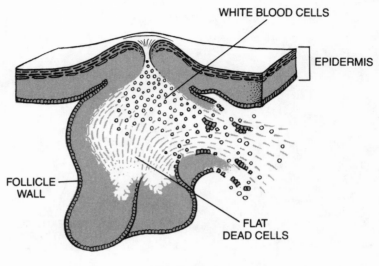

WHITE BLOOD CELLS

EPIDERMIS

FOLLICLE
WALL

FLAT
DEAD CELLS

Pustule

pustule. The skin over the pustule is thin, and eventually it may open, so that the pus drains out; or the white blood cells patrolling the tissues may clean up all the pus and carry it away, digesting it as they continue their patrols through the body. Papules and pustules are what we normally think of as "pimples."

BATTLE SCARS
When foreign material gets into the dermis and causes inflammation, some of the connective tissue is damaged. If all goes well, new tissue will form to replace the damaged tissue, and the skin will be as good as new. However, sometimes the repair is not complete, and a hole will be left in the dermis. Epidermis grows to cover the hole, and a depressed scar is formed.

Scarring is all the more probable when the break in the follicle wall is a large one. Then a lot of sebum, dead cells, and bacteria flood into the dermis, creating a large red bump, called a *nodule.* This is actually a larger form of the papule, and it feels firm. You may be tempted to squeeze it, hoping that the "bad stuff" will pop out and the pimple will heal. Instead, squeezing probably will just make the scarring worse.

The body's defenses work hard to get rid of the irritating material of the nodule. After a painful flare-up that may last for up to a week or so, the nodule may gradually subside into a papule, which in turn may take some weeks to disappear. If the accumulation of bacteria and cell matter is very large, the contents of the nodule may become enclosed inside a makeshift wall below the skin surface. Now the lesion has become a *cyst,* which may grow to as much as an inch in diameter. Pus builds up inside the cyst, making it feel somewhat soft. It may be red and throbbing, an "angry-looking" boil. A cyst will heal faster if it is opened, so that the contents can drain; but this is definitely *not* a do-it-yourself project. Opening a cyst is actually surgery, and it should be done by a doctor or other medical professional with special precautions to stop the bleeding, prevent further infection, and minimize scarring.

When the acne process progresses to cysts, the inflammation is usually very serious. The sebaceous gland in these large lesions is destroyed, and oil will never be produced in that spot again. Cysts can be painful, and

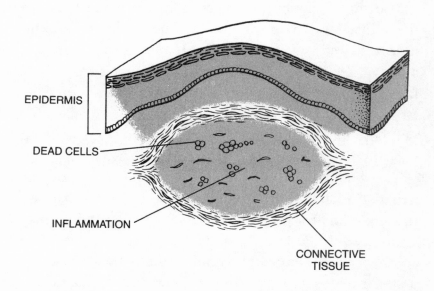

EPIDERMIS

DEAD CELLS

INFLAMMATION

CONNECTIVE TISSUE

Cyst

scarring often occurs, so you should see a dermatologist if your acne is this serious.

Many people never get papules, pustules, nodules, or cysts because their follicle walls are strong and the pore is always forced open, creating a blackhead, before the wall can give way. Other people almost never get blackheads but have a lot of inflamed lesions. This is because their follicle walls are not as strong. Unfortunately, there isn't much you can do to strengthen your follicle walls. You can't build them up with special exercises or salves or vitamins. Their strength is just something you're born with. The same goes for scarring. Some people's skin heals better than others'. Chance is also a big factor in scarring. If the follicle wall breaks close to the surface and if the break is small, there usually won't be any scarring. But if it is a large break, deep in the dermis, chances are that scarring will occur.

MORE PROBLEMS

In some people the repair process is too good! Sometimes too much connective tissue is created to replace the damaged tissue, creating a raised surface instead of a pitted hole. This is called a *keloid scar,* and it seems to be more comon in black people.

Open and closed comedones, papules, pustules, nodules, and cysts are not the only kinds of lesions that can develop. A *secondary comedo* is formed when a wall grows around the material that spills into the dermis through a broken follicle wall. This results in odd-shaped follicles. Other times, after the follicle wall ruptures, it grows toward another damaged follicle and the two walls join, creating a closed comedo with two openings. This can also happen with several follicles, creating a *polyporous comedo*. If this comedo bursts again and inflammation occurs, it can be rather serious because of all the built-up material that escapes. Pus may form and drain for a long time, creating what is called a *sinus tract*.

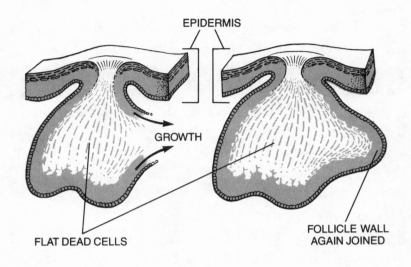

EPIDERMIS

GROWTH

FLAT DEAD CELLS

FOLLICLE WALL
AGAIN JOINED

Secondary comedo

THE ACNE BACTERIA

Another important factor in the development of acne is the bacteria that live on the skin. The normal skin microflora, as we have seen, includes many different kinds of bacteria, some of which help to protect us from other harmful microorganisms. But even these helpful bacteria can cause problems if they reproduce too much.

Sudden changes in the environment in which bacteria live can dramatically affect their microscopic communities. If the conditions become unfavorable for a particular type of bacteria, fewer of them will reproduce; if conditions become more favorable, more of them will be formed. When the body starts producing more

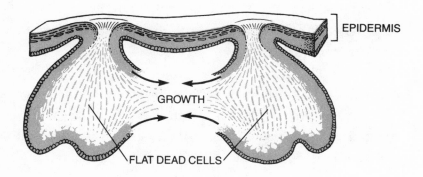

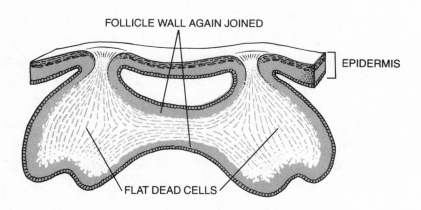

Polyporous comedo

sebum, this is a major change in the bacterial environment! One particular type of bacteria that seems to be common on the skin and in the follicles of people with acne is *Corynebacterium acnes* (abbreviated *C. acnes* and sometimes called *Propionibacterium acnes*.) Unlike most bacteria, which live on sugars, this bacterium feeds on the sebum produced by the sebaceous glands and produces fatty acids as a waste product. Unfortunately, this oily material is irritating to the skin and can aggravate an acne condition.

C. acnes bacteria do not grow as well in an open comedo because they prefer conditions that are anaerobic, which means an environment that has as little oxygen as possible. Closed comedones provide an ideal environment for them. There they reproduce rapidly and produce more of the irritating fatty acids. If a closed comedo containing many *C. acnes* bacteria ruptures and empties its contents into the dermis, real problems occur. The oil irritates and damages connective tissue, causing inflammation and infection that could lead to eventual scarring.

One thing to emphasize is that acne is *not* a contagious disease, transmitted by microbes, that one person can catch from another. The bacteria that are involved are normal inhabitants of the skin that become troublesome only when favorable conditions permit them to multiply excessively in the follicles. So you don't need to fear that you will develop acne if you touch, share food with, or kiss someone who has it.

4

Why Me?
Acne's Causes
and Aggravators

Most of the people who get acne are teenagers. But infants can get acne, too. Even unborn babies in the womb can get acne. (This is called *perinatal acne*.) People can get acne for the first time at age twenty, thirty, forty, fifty, even older. Why?

As we've already mentioned, no one yet knows for sure exactly why acne starts. But for as long as acne has been around, people have been speculating on what causes acne or makes it worse. Things that cause acne are said to be *acnegenic,* or *comedogenic* (producing co-medones). Some of the speculations sound logical enough but actually have turned out to be wrong.

ACNE MYTHS

One of the earliest beliefs about acne was that it was caused by dirt—the result of not keeping the skin properly cleaned. Many people still believe this, but it isn't so. It *is* important to clean the skin regularly, because dirt and excess oil on the skin may contribute to blocking pores and slowing down the flow of sebum out to the surface. But dirt does not cause skin cells to clump together and cling to the follicle walls. That happens deep inside the follicle, where cleaning can't reach.

Another long held belief about acne was that it was somehow related to sex. "Don't worry," people would tell a teenaged boy or girl worrying about pimples. "When you get married, your skin will clear up." The idea that sexual activity could help cure acne also made a good line for someone trying to persuade a reluctant date to "fool around." Paradoxically, acne has also been associated with having too much sex. That idea got started because people noticed that acne usually occurs during adolescence—the time when a person is becoming sexually mature. (The ancient Greeks were the first to link acne and adolescence, about twenty-five hundred years ago.) Some medical authorities suggested that masturbation was an important cause of acne—a notion that was especially popular during the repressive Victorian era. Such misconceptions about acne and sex persisted until the 1940s, when scientific studies established that sexual activity and acne are not related.

DO FOODS CAUSE ACNE?

Perhaps the most popular idea links acne breakouts to diet. Doctors used to tell their patients to avoid certain foods thought to cause acne. However, over the years so many different foods have been called acnegenic that a person who avoided them all would have practically nothing left to eat. The most notorious acnegenic foods were thought to be chocolate, colas, and greasy foods such as French fries and potato chips. Today most doctors do not feel that diet plays a very important role in acne breakouts. They point to studies of patients who ate large quantities of chocolates or peanuts and did not break out afterwards as proof that diet does not affect acne.

The topic of diet and acne, however, is still under debate. Some doctors claim that the effect of foods should not be ruled out just because a breakout does not occur immediately after eating a possible acnegenic food. Pimples can take weeks or even months to develop. How, then, can we be sure something eaten now will not cause a breakout of pimples several days or weeks from now?

Many doctors who do feel diet has a role in the development of acne have noticed some of their patients had definite breakouts after eating chocolate, sugar, or greasy foods. Others answer that only sensitive people break out after eating these foods. They point to studies such as one that found one out of four people are sensitive to chocolate and may have an acnelike reaction to it. These doctors claim that the reaction is not really acne at all, but rather an allergic reaction that is mistaken for the common acne vulgaris.

Foods that contain iodides have also been linked with acne. Many shellfish are high in iodides. So are pretzels and potato chips, which contain iodized salt. Gluten bread has also been blamed. Excess amounts of iodides probably contribute to the acne process by making the response of the white blood cells to inflammation less effective. But not all doctors agree that iodides are major contributors to acne. Some claim that the levels required to cause breakouts are very high, and normal eating habits would not pose a problem.

Many doctors avoid the debate about acne and food and simply advise their patients to stay away from any foods that seem to cause a problem. If a breakout occurs, they suggest, stay away from the food for a while. Then, after the flare-up goes away, try it again. If the problem recurs, this is a food you should avoid. This is a highly individual matter, to be determined by each person by trial and error.

HORMONES AND PUBERTY

The question of hormones is even more complex. There is no doubt that the hormones secreted by an adolescent's body play a role in acne.

The fact that acne usually occurs at puberty, when sex hormones are released into the bloodstream in large quantities, suggests a definite connection between acne and increased levels of *androgens,* the normal male sex hormones. Eunuchs—men whose testes have been removed or destroyed—do not produce testosterone. Although some androgens are produced by the adrenal glands, their overall levels are low, like those of a child before puberty. It's no coincidence that eunuchs don't get acne.

Flare-ups of acne in adolescent girls and women are also linked with sex steroid hormones. Typically, pimples peak during menstrual periods, and that is when a woman's progesterone levels are highest. (Progesterone is chemically very similar to the main androgen, testosterone.)

However, as some research has revealed, higher androgen levels in the blood do not necessarily mean more oil will be produced in the skin. Actually, people with oily skin and a tendency to develop acne usually have normal levels of androgens in their bodies. And though the testosterone level remains high in an adult man, most boys do eventually outgrow acne after puberty has ended. So the level of the sex hormones is not the only important factor. What counts is how sensitive the sebaceous glands are to the androgens that are present.

Some people's sebaceous glands are more sensitive than others'. Even in a person's own body, sebaceous glands differ in their androgen sensitivity. For example, most people's skin is oilier in the center of the face than anywhere else. The areas on the forehead, nose, cheeks around the nose, and the chin are usually oilier even in people with normal skin and no acne problems. This is because the sebaceous glands in this area are larger and more sensitive than those in other places. Doctors call this sensitivity *end-organ sensitivity*. Heredity plays an important role in determining each person's end-organ sensitivity.

WHO GETS ACNE?

Increased oil production is obviously related to acne breakouts. But why does acne start? Heredity probably plays an important role in who gets acne and how severe the case will be. However, unlike other conditions that are very rare, acne is so common—nearly everyone gets it—that it is hard to determine how much of a role heredity plays. Some people whose parents had severe cases of acne develop severe cases of their own. Others don't.

Geography and culture are also uncertain factors. Before white people brought modern ways to Alaska, conditions such as heart disease and acne were very rare among the Eskimos. Now there are many more cases. Did diet play the major role? Was it the change in lifestyle? Research has not yet brought a definite answer.

WHAT CAUSES ACNE?

One current theory about acne has to do with the bacteria that live on the skin and in the follicles, particularly *C. acnes*. Research has shown that the fatty acids produced by these bacteria sometimes act to speed up the turnover rate of skin cells in the epidermis. New cells are produced in the basal layer at a faster rate. They displace the older cells, pushing them outward and causing more dead outer epidermal cells to be formed. This is a defense mechanism, producing a thicker layer of dead cells as a shield to protect the body. Some scientists feel this might be part of a chain reaction contributing to the start of acne: An increase in the oil production in the skin feeds the *C. acnes* bacteria present there and creates a population explosion of these microbes. The multiplying bacteria produce more fatty acids, which irritate the skin and prompt it to produce more dead cells. This combination of extra cells and extra oil could set the stage for acne.

Another idea about acne is that the pore openings in an adolescent's skin are not big enough to handle the increased amount of oil. The pores are still immature and cannot accommodate the growth spurts that the body experiences at this time. This immature pore size makes it more difficult for the sebum to flow. Things get backed up inside, as the body produces more and more oil, and more dead cells are sloughed off inside the follicle. Eventually the pores grow bigger, and the sebum can flow more freely—but this often takes years.

But what about adults who get acne? How does this fit in with the "too-small-pore-size" theory? Dermatologists find that 60 percent of their patients with acne are adult women. In fact, some doctors suggest that between 30 and 50 percent of all adult women have acne flare-ups at one time or another. Many dermatologists believe that the biggest cause of acne in adult women is the cosmetics they use. Makeup foundations and moisturizers are often oily or greasy and can clog the pore openings, causing *acne cosmetica*. Pores clogged with oily makeup are similar to the immature pore openings in adolescents. In both cases the flow of sebum is restricted, which can contribute to a backup inside the follicle. Cosmetics manufacturers dispute this theory, contending that most cosmetic products sold to the public are nonacnegenic. Recently dermatologists and cosmetic-industry researchers have been reviewing the results of testing in a cooperative attempt to resolve the question.

Probably both mechanisms—a bacterial population explosion fueled by increased oil production and a clogging of follicles whose pores are too small to permit a free flow of sebum—contribute to the acne process. Perhaps other factors will be discovered. When scientists find out for sure exactly *why* acne happens, a "cure" for acne will be only one step away. For now, though, dealing with acne means learning about as many things that can cause acne (or acnelike conditions) as possible. If you know what may trigger your acne breakouts, you may be able to minimize acne problems.

SUN, HEAT, AND HUMIDITY

Many people find their acne gets better in the summer, while some find it gets worse. For the people whose problems improve, the answer seems to be the greater exposure to sunlight, whose ultraviolet rays can kill bacteria. Sunlight also promotes increased scaling, as the skin thickens protectively and the dead outer layers flake off more rapidly. This scaling can help unblock clogged pores. So doctors used to advise moderate sunbathing or treatments with UV lamps to help clear up acne.

But recently, medical specialists have become more aware of the negative effects of sun exposure. Ultraviolet light is powerful. If it is strong enough to kill bacteria, you might wonder what it can do to your skin. For one thing, it can produce chemical changes in the skin protein collagen. The long chemical chains of this protein get linked together rigidly, instead of providing an elastic framework. Gradually the skin becomes wrinkled, tough, and leathery—old looking. Even worse, the UV rays can strike deep into the skin cells, producing changes in the chemicals that guide and control their activities. Such a changed skin cell may suddenly run wild, multiplying uncontrollably and producing a cancerous growth. A suntan is the body's defense against UV rays: The dark pigment melanin soaks up the radiation harmlessly and shields the more delicate structures in the cells. A sunburn means that you were exposed to more sun than you were equipped to handle; dermatologists now believe that most skin cancers can be traced back to a sunburn some time in the past.

Doctors today warn against overdoing sunbathing as an acne remedy, and they frown on UV lamps. You should always use a sunscreen when out in the sun, one that blocks out the UV rays effectively. But beware of oily ones that can aggravate acne problems by blocking pores. Alcohol-based sunscreens are better for your skin than oily, greasy ones, since alcohol helps to clean off excess oil and dirt.

The summer sun may be beneficial to the skin, but coupled with humidity, summer heat can cause acne to get worse. Skin cells swell in hot, humid weather, and this can block the follicles, preventing sebum from flowing properly and causing acne breakouts.

In some severe cases, *tropical acne* can develop. Large nodules and cysts form on the shoulders and back where the skin is rubbed by clothing. This sometimes happens to soldiers, for example, who are stationed in hot, tropical climates and have to do a lot of physical labor. Some research has suggested that a yeast called *Pityrosporum ovale* may be involved in tropical acne cases.

In hot, humid weather, it might be advisable to use an astringent (a lotion that dries and tightens the skin) a few times a day to remove excess oil. One good thing about astringents is that they come in medicated pads that you can take along anywhere. They can be stashed in a gym bag, purse, or knapsack for use at times when soap-and-water washing isn't possible.

PRESSURE AND OTHER AGGRAVATORS

During the summer, remember to reduce friction against the skin, which can also cause acne. Sitting in a vinyl seat in a car, at home, or at work can cause sweat to accumulate. The same is true of exercising in tight-fitting, nonabsorbent clothes. Moreover, friction produced by rubbing against the chair or by rough clothes rubbing against the body can damage follicles swollen and blocked by humidity. Headbands, backpack straps, and football helmet straps all can cause flare-ups when they touch and rub on the skin, even in cold climates.

Some doctors believe that pressure on the skin alone can cause problems. If you lean your chin on your hand while studying, for example, you may have an acne breakout on your chin. Apparently pressure locks moisture into the skin, causing the surface layer around the pores to swell. This makes the pore openings smaller, so the oil cannot escape properly. Acne that is caused by rubbing, friction, or pressure on the skin is *acne mechanica*. Placing a towel on the chair, wearing loose, absorbent clothes, using talcum powder, and keeping as little pressure on the skin as possible are good ways to minimize problems.

Acne can be aggravated by anything that prevents sebum from flowing freely through the follicle and out onto the surface of the skin. Some people find that if they wear their hair in bangs, they break out on the forehead. People with long hair sometimes get acne on the neck and upper back. This is caused by the oils from the hair, which may help to clog the pore openings, and possibly by friction of the hair rubbing on the skin.

*Over*cleaning your face can also worsen acne pimples

and result in what doctors call *acne detergicans*. Some people scrub very hard and use abrasive cleansers to try to scrub acne away. Sometimes this overcleaning can irritate plugged-up follicles, causing them to rupture and become inflamed. Instead of washing away the acne, it only makes the area more raw and worse than before.

Acne can also be caused by a person's work environment. *Occupational acne* is what sometimes happens when the skin is exposed to a lot of oil or grease on the job. Some people who work in fast-food restaurants, for example, can develop severe cases of acne if they are constantly exposed to splattering oil and grease in a kitchen. Machinists and mechanics, too, may develop acne on their arms from constant exposure to oil and grease.

Sometimes medications the doctor prescribes for an illness can cause acne pimples as a side effect. *Acne medicamentosa* is the name for this type of breakout. Steroids and drugs used to control epileptic seizures can sometimes cause acne. So can oral contraceptives. Lithium, phenobarbital, and Dilantin can cause breakouts. Some cough and cold medicines or multivitamins that contain bromides and iodides are sometimes culprits. Danazol, a synthetic androgen used to treat endometriosis, and INH, an anti-TB drug, have sometimes caused eruptions. Excessive amounts of vitamin B_{12} can also cause breakouts.

Usually breakouts caused by medications will look

different from ordinary acne problems. Steroid eruptions, for example, most often occur as a number of small, shallow pustules. If you suspect that a medication you are taking is causing breakouts, don't stop taking it on your own. Discuss it with your doctor. He or she will examine the pimples, and if the medication seems to be causing you to break out, perhaps another drug will be substituted for it.

Some people notice that the area around the mouth is particularly prone to acne. The culprit may be toothpaste. Some people react to the fluoride in the toothpaste by breaking out in acne pimples. If you think this might be your problem, try a nonfluoridated toothpaste for a while to see if the skin in the area clears up. Soaps used to wash the skin may also contribute to acne if they contain oily cleansing cream or fragrance. (Some people are sensitive to perfumes.)

Sometimes breakouts can occur when something is missing from your diet. Some people break out when their bodies do not have enough vitamin C, for example.

Men with curly hair may develop a particular kind of acne problem. Their facial hairs are curly, too, and the tips may turn back into the pores and become ingrown, causing acnelike pimples. This condition is called *pseudofolliculitis barbae*. It is often worsened by shaving.

Some people are affected by foods and drinks that cause the blood vessels to expand. These are called *vasodilators*. Spicy foods and hot drinks such as coffee and tea, as well as alcoholic drinks, are all vasodilators, which cause the face to be flushed. People with an acnelike condition called *acne rosacea* are particularly sensitive to vasodilators. The capillaries beneath the skin become enlarged and sometimes are damaged, causing the nose and surrounding area to be puffy and red. Pimples break out on and around the nose, as well as on the cheeks and forehead, and the area around the pimples is red and inflamed. Acne rosacea usually occurs in people over thirty, particularly in women, although men who have the condition often have more severe cases. W. C. Fields was one famous acne rosacea sufferer. Sometimes this condition is called "whiskey nose," but this is an unfair description; although alcohol can worsen the problem, acne rosacea also occurs in people who have never had a drink in their lives. Severe cases of acne rosacea require treatment with prescription drugs: antibiotics or the recently approved metronidazole, which comes in a water-based gel form that is colorless and odorless and can be used under makeup.

STRESS AND ACNE

Having acne breakouts when you're under a lot of pressure or stress is rather common. Emotions and stress can have a great effect on the condition of your body. Anger causes blood to rush to the head and the heart to beat faster. Panic can cause dizziness, nausea, chest pains, and heart palpitations. Stress can lead to rapid heartbeat, anxiety attacks, and loss of appetite. It can even contribute to heart disease and cancer. Stress and other emotions can also affect your skin.

Stress stimulates the adrenal glands. These glands produce the hormone cortisone, which stimulates the sebaceous gland to produce more oil—and that, of course, helps set the stage for acne problems. Stress also lowers the body's resistance to bacteria and viruses, by causing the disease-fighting cells of the immune system to work less efficiently. These lowered immune defenses leave you easy prey to colds and other illnesses and can also contribute to acne breakouts by letting the acne bacteria multiply unhindered.

People who are worried or under pressure often absentmindedly pick at their pimples. But this can be harmful, increasing the likelihood of infection and in the long run making the acne longer lasting, more severe, and more likely to result in scarring. Realizing that you pick at your pimples and forcing yourself to stop can be very helpful in clearing up acne.

Stress can never be completely avoided, but controlling the amount of stress in your life can affect your whole body's health, including that of the skin. You can do many things to reduce stress. Regular exercise helps to release tensions instead of letting them build up inside. It's important to get enough sleep and be well rested. When your body is tired, your resistance is greatly lowered. Proper vitamin intake from a balanced diet (or vitamin supplements) is also important for maintaining the body's resistance. Some research has shown that proper levels of vitamins A, B, C, and E and the minerals zinc and selenium can help keep the body's defenses strong.

Countless psychological factors contribute to stress— and can contribute to acne. When you set impossible goals for yourself, you may be causing yourself unnecessary stress. Bottling up things that bother you can also cause stress to build up. It's almost always better to talk things out than to keep them inside.

Now you know some of the causes of acne. You should have a better idea of things to avoid in order to minimize acne problems. But more than likely, even if you avoid all the possible acnegenic factors, still you'll have some acne. If your acne is severe, you should not delay, but see a doctor as soon as possible. The earlier you start treating severe acne, the less likely you are to have complications—such as scars.

If you're like most people, though, you'll probably want to try to tackle your acne problem on your own. But when you go to the drugstore, you will find a confusing assortment of acne remedies. They all claim to be good for acne. How do you decide which is best for you? You've already learned what acne is and how pimples start and progress. Now you need to understand how acne medications work.

5

Tackling Pimples on Your Own

Someday, waking up to find a pimple on your face won't merit more than a momentary shrug. You'll just take a pill or rub in a dab of cream, and—*poof!*—the pimple will be gone. Unfortunately, that day hasn't arrived yet. The treatments available today will usually make pimples go away, but it will probably take days— even weeks or more, contrary to what television commercials suggest.

If you're like most teenagers, before you decide to seek professional help from your family doctor or a dermatologist, you'll probably want to try one of the over-the-counter medications you've heard about. You won't have any trouble finding one at your drugstore or supermarket—at least three hundred acne remedies are on the market! Americans currently spend more than $175 million each year on over-the-counter acne remedies.

To most people, fighting acne means grabbing the tube of medication you keep in the medicine cabinet whenever one of those ugly pimples pops up. You rub it in desperately, hoping the pimple will vanish. More than likely, you will be very disappointed.

If your acne is only a mild case, you might shrug and try to live with your pimples, figuring there's nothing you can really do, anyway. But you'd be wrong there, too. The acne remedies you can buy over the counter *can* be effective for most people, if they are used correctly.

Doctors say the reason many people find acne medications ineffective is that they don't use them properly. Acne medications should not be rubbed only on the pimples, but on the entire area where acne occurs. For every pimple you can see, others are just starting and are not yet visible. (Remember, pimples can take weeks to develop.) Some doctors think that if you stick to a daily cleaning routine, followed by the application of one of the acne medications, not only will it clear up your skin, it will actually minimize future breakouts! Now that's a good reason to begin a plan of attack on acne as soon as possible.

CLEANING IS THE WAY TO START

Cleaning your skin properly before you apply an acne medication can help it to work more effectively. Thorough cleaning with soap and water helps remove excess oil, dirt, and dead skin cells. Many medicated soaps contain sulfur, salicylic acid, or benzoyl peroxide, ingredients that kill bacteria and soften and peel dead skin. Should you use one of them? Some doctors suggest that although these products can be helpful for many people, soaps do not usually stay on the skin long enough for the "medication" in them to sink into the pores. If you are using an acne medication such as benzoyl peroxide, the extra medication in the soap may be unnecessary.

Abrasive cleansers contain gritty particles that work to gently irritate the skin. They rough away dead skin cells by scratching away some of the outer layers. They can be quite helpful for people with stubborn acne problems. Often they may help get rid of pimples faster. Some people, though, find that abrasive cleansers, pads, and brushes irritate the skin too much. Sometimes the irritation can rupture follicles, causing inflammation and even making the acne worse.

Another useful cleaning product is a facial mask. It is applied in the form of a cream or lotion, which is left on for fifteen minutes or more while the face is soaked with moist cloths or steamed to open the pores. The facial mask can help to clean away dead skin cells deeper than normal cleaning. However, if you use one of these facial masks, you should remember it will make your skin more sensitive to acne medications, because the medication will penetrate deeper—there isn't as much "shield" to protect the body. Some cleansing masks combine acne medication with a facial mask.

Some doctors suggest to their patients that a mild, fragrance-free soap is really all they need when washing is combined with using an acne medication. Choosing the right cleaning product is something you will have to decide, in light of your own personal preferences as well as the sensitivity of your skin.

How often should you wash your face? Too much washing can actually be bad. Dermatologists generally suggest that twice a day in the winter and three times a day in summer is sufficient. You should use warm water—never hot, which causes the blood vessels in the skin to expand and can add to inflammation. After you gently lather in the soap with your fingertips, you should rinse it off completely. Some doctors suggest rinsing with warm water ten times or more to make sure all soap residue is gone. Then pat dry with an absorbent towel, and your face (or other affected area) is ready for the acne medication.

DECISIONS, DECISIONS . . .

Going to the store to buy an acne remedy can be a little overwhelming. There are so many different products of so many different types! You can choose from countless numbers of *medicated soaps, astringents* (which are usually alcohol-based for cleaning off excess oil and dirt), *abrasive cleansers* and *abrasive pads* and *brushes* (which work to scrub off the outer layers of your skin very much like the scouring pads you use on pots and pans), acne *creams* and *lotions,* and acne *cover-up* products. How are you supposed to know what you really need?

You can ask other people what worked or didn't work for them. Unfortunately, what works for some people doesn't always work for others. And if someone else didn't use the product properly, his or her opinion may not be valid. The best thing to do is to understand how these different types of products work and what the differences are, take into account your own personal factors—such as how sensitive your skin is—and choose a course of action. Try it out and see how it works. If it works, stick with it. If it doesn't, try something else.

As you now know, acne is caused by sebum and dead cells clumping together and sticking to the follicle walls as well as by the irritating effects of an overpopulation of bacteria. Acne medications try to counteract the acne process by combating one or both of these factors.

BENZOYL PEROXIDE: THE OVER-THE-COUNTER CHAMP

Many of the acne products of the past contained drugs such as alcohol, resorcinol, salicylic acid, and sulfur as their main ingredients. These drugs were not very effective, and they tended to irritate sensitive skin. Then in the mid-1970s, a drug that had been discovered in the 1920s was tested on acne patients. The results were so dramatic that now the drug—benzoyl peroxide—is the most widely used over-the-counter acne medication and the one most often recommended by dermatologists.

Benzoyl peroxide works in two ways to fight acne. It kills bacteria, and it causes a mild drying and peeling of the skin.

A "peroxide" is a chemical that contains extra oxygen—more than the usual amount. Peroxides tend to be rather reactive compounds, giving up their extra oxygen at the slightest provocation. When you apply a benzoyl peroxide product to your skin, it seeps down into the follicle. It encounters a variety of natural body chemicals on the way, and chemical reactions occur, releasing oxygen. But the bacteria that produce the oily substance that irritates the skin prefer to live in anaerobic conditions where there is little or no oxygen. The oxygen released from the benzoyl peroxide kills many of the bacteria.

As benzoyl peroxide soaks into the skin and seeps into the follicles, it also produces another important effect. It loosens the dead skin cells that have clumped to the follicle walls, allowing them to be washed away in the flow of sebum. Of course, you can't see that happening, but your skin will look drier and will gently peel for at least the first month. The technical name for something that causes the skin to peel is an *exfoliant*. Why would you want your skin to peel? Actually, it isn't the peeling effect you can see that is helping to clear up your acne but rather the peeling that is happening on a microscopic scale, down inside the follicles.

Not everyone can use benzoyl peroxide. Some find it too irritating, especially those with very fair complexions. Others develop an allergy to benzoyl peroxide and begin to have reactions after using it successfully for a while. Black people and Asians should be especially careful because the peeling effects sometimes cause unwanted dark spots in people whose skin can produce large amounts of melanin. Many acne sufferers must resort to a product that may be less effective—one that contains sulfur or salicylic acid, for example.

Benzoyl peroxide medications come in various forms: lotions, creams, and gels. Gels seem to be most effective, but they are usually available only by prescription. Benzoyl peroxide products also come in different strengths—5-percent and 10-percent solutions. The more sensitive your skin, the lower the percentage you should use. You should always work up slowly to determine how much you should use and how often you need to apply it.

You may find benzoyl peroxide irritating at first, but in time your body may be able to get used to it. One doctor's suggestion, and perhaps the safest approach, is to start out using the medication once a day, before you go to sleep each night. Rub it gently over the whole area where acne pimples occur, not just on the pimples themselves. Wash the medication off after fifteen minutes the first night. Then, over a week, gradually increase the time you leave it on each night. By the end of the week you should be able to leave the medication on for the entire night. Then, in the morning, it should be washed off. Eventually you might want to work up to twice-a-day applications.

When using benzoyl peroxide, you should experience some amount of dryness and peeling. But if nothing happens, you may need to use a stronger solution or apply it more often or for longer periods of time. If too much dryness and peeling occur, decrease the strength or number of applications.

SOME SPECIAL CAUTIONS

Remember when using acne medications not to get them in or around your eyes or lips, or in your nose or mouth. Some people find medications are particularly irritating to the neck, so apply them there with caution if you have acne in that area.

There are some important things to remember when using benzoyl peroxide. Like hydrogen peroxide, it can bleach hair and clothes. So be sure not to get any on your good clothing. Many people find it's best to wear a white T-shirt to bed, particularly if you are putting the medication on your neck or back. Also be careful when you are in the sun. The sun itself causes a mild peeling, and if sunlight is combined with the medication, peeling can occur at a much higher rate. The results can be quite uncomfortable!

Remember, too, that for the first month almost everyone experiences some amount of mild "hotness" in the area being treated. However, if the medication causes severe burning feelings and your skin becomes red and inflamed, you should stop using benzoyl peroxide immediately. About one in twenty people are allergic to this drug.

Benzoyl peroxide is sensitive to heat, which causes the drug to lose its strength as some of the reactive peroxide breaks down. Therefore, you should keep it in the refrigerator.

After your skin gets used to benzoyl peroxide, you might want to work up to a higher strength—to 10 percent, for example—or apply it more often. However, be sure to work up slowly to any new strength.

STAYING ACNE-FREE

After one to three months of using benzoyl peroxide in a regular daily treatment, most people find their acne greatly improved, and many find that new breakouts occur much less often. For best results you should try not to miss a day in treatment. You don't want to give the acne process any chance to begin forming new block-ups in the follicles.

Even after the acne seems to be gone, you can't just relax and forget about it. Experts suggest you continue using the acne medication at a lower "maintenance" level. There are no cures for acne. Your pimples may be gone for the moment, but you still have all your follicles, and your body is still producing oil. In time, your population of *C. acnes* will start multiplying all over again. So if you stop applying the acne medications, acne will more than likely flare up again. Until your body conditions change, you have the best chance of staying acne-free if you stick to a regular program of cleaning and medication.

TO PICK OR NOT TO PICK?

Picking at pimples and popping "zits" is a sensitive issue. Almost everyone is guilty of popping a pimple at one time or another. Some kinds of lesions may actually heal faster when they are drained. Blackheads, for example, which are open to the surface, can be carefully drained. Soaking your skin with a wet washcloth first can help to soften the material in the pores and make them easier to drain. The trick is never to squeeze too hard and to stop if the pore does not empty easily. You have to be *very* careful not to force any material down into the skin. This could cause the follicle to rupture, producing inflammation. Drugstores sell comedo extractors designed for "popping" these pimples. However, many dermatologists suggest that their patients should leave all lesions alone. Picking and scratching and popping can lead to inflammation and infection, which could cause scars where ordinary pimples would have healed without a trace. If pimples really bother you,

you should let a dermatologist drain the lesions. He or she will know the safest way to minimize problems.

Some people really cannot help themselves when it comes to picking at their pimples. It becomes an obsession. *Acne excoria* occurs in those individuals who actually dig out every tiny bump that flares up under the skin. This causes scabs and inflammation, which prompt more picking. The result, unfortunately, is often permanent scarring.

HOW TO TELL IF YOU NEED MORE HELP

Many people find it hard to judge just how much improvement has taken place during treatment. It's very much like going on a diet. The people who see you every day may not notice any change at all, because it is a gradual process. But someone who hasn't seen you in a while will surely notice a difference.

One trick for evaluating your progress in treating acne is to take a picture of your face before you begin treatment. Another is to count the number of lesions. Remember to stretch the skin and look for closed comedones, which may otherwise be hidden. Eventually they may erupt as blackheads or pimples, and you may think your condition has gotten worse when actually the new pimples only came from closed comedones that were already there. Once a week, recount the different types of lesions.

Unfortunately benzoyl peroxide, which is the best over-the-counter treatment, is more effective in clearing up lesions that have progressed to the papule and pustule stage—actual pimples—than in clearing up comedones. More effective treatments can be prescribed by a physician.

If the results of your self-treatment are not evident after three months, it might be advisable to see a dermatologist. If you do, tell the doctor exactly what treatments you have been using, and what the results have been. This may be important information in deciding on the best approach for treating your particular condition.

6

Seeing a Dermatologist

Ten percent of the people with acne decide their condition is just too much to handle alone, and they go to see a skin specialist.

The first meeting with the dermatologist is a sort of get-acquainted visit. The doctor will examine your skin and, just as important, will ask you a series of questions. Both these approaches help to give the doctor a picture of your problem—the kind of knowledge that will be needed to determine what kind of treatment might work best for you.

DIAGNOSING YOUR ACNE PROBLEM

In the first visit, you will be asked to describe your condition as completely as you can: how long you've had it, whether it goes in cycles of getting better and worse, whether you've noticed some special trigger for breakouts. The doctor will want to know what treatments you have tried for acne breakouts and how well they worked. You'll be asked if there is a lot of stress in your life and whether you are taking any medications such as cold medicines or birth control pills.

The information you supply will help to determine what kind of acne problem you have—common acne (acne vulgaris) or breakouts caused by something else (cosmetics, greases, allergic reactions, medications, and so on).

The second checkpoint is "How severe is your acne?" There are three general classes of severity: mild, moderate, and severe. If you have papules that have not turned into pustules, and a few comedones, the doctor will probably classify your case as *mild*. In a *moderate* case of acne, papules, pustules, and inflamed red areas will be present. When there are papules, pustules, and cysts, the acne case is *severe*.

SELECTING A TREATMENT

Once the doctor has determined how severe your acne is, the next step is to prescribe a treatment. Unfortunately, what works for some people doesn't necessarily work for others, and the only way to tell if a particular treatment will work for *you* is to try it out and see whether it helps.

Sometimes after starting a treatment, the patient and doctor will find that that particular medication causes too much irritation or other side effects, and it has to be stopped. (It's not always possible to predict in advance whether a drug will have side effects, because people vary greatly in their reactions to medications. You might turn out to be very sensitive to a substance that does not bother most people.)

The dermatologist may prescribe several medications at the same time. The drugs attack different parts of the problem, or work in different ways, so that their combined effect may be much greater than that of each medication alone. The doctor may start the treatment with several different drugs at once, or add more drugs gradually.

Bringing acne under control is a very individual matter, with the approach tailor made for each patient. So the doctor may have to try several different treatments before finding the right one. Any acne treatment will usually take several months to produce results that will satisfy you.

STARTING YOUR TREATMENT

Typically, in mild acne cases, a doctor will start out with a *topical medication*—one that is rubbed into the skin. Usually a *benzoyl peroxide* solution will be used (like the over-the-counter ones, but often stronger and more effective). If you've already tried an over-the-counter benzoyl peroxide solution, be sure to tell the doctor what results it produced. This information may help in your treatment.

The doctor will check your particular skin type to determine the correct treatment for you. In addition to the many types of drugs available, there are different bases (vehicles) that a drug can be mixed in, and some bases are better than others for different skin types. For example, an alcohol base is best when the skin is particularly oily. If a person's skin is easily irritated, a gel base may be used. In addition, different companies may use the same drug but add varying combinations of other ingredients that may be less or more irritating to different skin types.

The doctor will explain exactly how the medication is to be used. You will be told to use the medication sparingly—applying more medication doesn't necessarily mean that more of the drug will get *into* the skin, deep in the follicles where it does its job. Probably the doctor will start you out with one application a day, after washing and patting dry. Then once you become adjusted to the treatment, two or three times a day may be suggested. The doctor will ask you to record any irritations to your skin and at your next visit may recommend increasing or decreasing the strength of the medication. Remember, too, acne medications are meant to be used on the entire area where acne occurs, not just on the pimples that are there now. (But be sure to avoid the areas around the eyes and mouth.) The doctor will also stress the importance of using an acne medication every day—missing a day may give the acne a chance to produce a new flare-up. Usually there should be noticeable differences after about two months.

FINE TUNING

Typically you will have a long initial visit with the dermatologist to determine what kind of problem you have and the best ways of treating it. Another visit will be scheduled for a month to six weeks later to check up on how well the treatment is working. Later checkups may be arranged after another month to six weeks, as needed.

If improvement is not satisfactory after two months, the doctor will probably have you continue using the benzoyl peroxide solution, but in addition an *antibiotic lotion* may be added to the treatment plan. Usually *erythromycin* or *clindamycin* is prescribed. They seem to work not only by killing bacteria but also by making the anti-inflammatory action of the white blood cells more effective. *Tetracycline* may be used, but some people are allergic to it. If clindamycin is prescribed, the doctor will remind you always to keep it refrigerated; otherwise it may not be effective. The antibiotic and benzoyl peroxide solution can be applied right on top of each other. Sometimes the doctor will prescribe a single medication, like Benzamycin, which combines both benzoyl peroxide and erythromycin (or another antibiotic) in one application.

In a moderate acne case, the doctor will start treatment with a combination therapy immediately. If a lot of comedones are present, the doctor may try an alternate approach, because benzoyl peroxide is not very effective on comedones. The treatment most often recommended when many comedones are present is *tretinoin* or *retinoic acid,* which is made from vitamin A. The trade name for the popular retinoic acid product manufactured by Ortho Pharmaceuticals is Retin-A. Its current gel and cream formulas are much less irritating than the form that was first available. As with other acne treatments, a good two months of retinoic acid applications are needed before any real results can be seen.

If your doctor prescribes Retin-A, you will be warned not to be alarmed if your acne seems to be getting *worse* at first. That's quite normal with retinoic acid treatments, because the drug works to speed up the acne process. It causes the comedones to erupt out of the follicles, clearing them. Other deeper, closed lesions leak into the dermis, as they would have eventually, but the treatment causes these events to happen at a much faster rate. So it seems as though you are getting more breakouts than usual, even while the drug is really helping you. Retin-A works by penetrating into the pores and loosening the dead cells that have clumped together. It also helps to slow down the growth of bacteria and to build up the weakened follicle walls. The result is that the dead cells do not clump together anymore, but instead are carried out with the sebum to the surface—just as they are supposed to be.

Most people find Retin-A somewhat irritating at first, but the skin usually adapts within a few days or weeks. This drug does, however, continue to make the skin much more sensitive to other irritants, such as harsh soaps, over-the-counter medications, or the menthol, lime, or spices that may be found in makeup or aftershave lotion. All these should be avoided during the Retin-A treatment. Applying the drug at bedtime helps to minimize discomfort.

In more serious acne cases with a lot of inflammation and many pustules, papules, and cysts, an *oral antibiotic* may be prescribed in addition to benzoyl peroxide and/ or Retin-A. Usually tetracycline is used, because this antibiotic (unlike some others) is generally safe when taken for long periods of time. Remember, though, never to use tetracycline that has been sitting around for a long time. Like other drugs, it gradually breaks down, and even one-year-old tetracycline may be not only ineffective but quite harmful, if not toxic.

Antibiotic treatments can have some bothersome side effects. They may make your skin more sensitive to sunlight, so that you need to avoid the sun or protect yourself with an effective sunblock before any exposure to the sun—not only at the beach but even at a ball game or in the garden. (An interesting, and somewhat embarrassing, side effect appears under black lights, like those found at discos or museums: If you are taking tetracycline, your skin may glow a yellowish-green color.) You should take antibiotics on an empty stomach, because certain foods can interfere with their absorption. (If you take a multivitamin, be sure to mention this to your doctor. The iron in the multivitamin can sometimes prevent tetracycline from being absorbed properly in the body.) Women may have special problems when they take antibiotics for extended periods of time. The drug kills off the microflora that normally lives in the delicate membranes lining the body openings, and hardier yeasts may multiply in the mouth or vagina, producing an irritating infection called candidiasis.

If tetracycline does not produce the right results, *erythromycin* is the next choice. And if that doesn't work, a more expensive antibiotic called *minocycline* may be used. When used in very low doses, minocycline is very effective for acne and has no serious side effects. (But it should not be taken during pregnancy—it stains the teeth of the developing baby green.)

A DANGEROUS CURE?

If nothing else works in a serious acne case, the doctor might suggest *isotretinoin,* or Accutane—but only as a last resort. Ninety percent of patients with severe cystic acne will be virtually cleared of acne problems after about five months of treatment with Accutane. And acne problems usually stay away for years after treatment is stopped. When this product first came out in 1982, it was the closest thing to a wonder drug for acne. But doctors knew it could cause some serious problems. Some of the side effects are lip and skin peeling, nosebleeds, nausea, headaches, and blurred vision.

That's not the worst of it. A few patients taking Accutane develop liver abnormalities. Triglyceride levels may build up in the body, and excessive levels of these fats in the blood can lead to heart disease. That's one reason why most dermatologists are very cautious about using Accutane. They usually require a signed consent before agreeing to prescribe it and give extensive blood tests before and during treatment to be sure no serious side effects are developing. Contact-lens users have to wear glasses if they take Accutane, because nearly everyone who uses the drug develops dry eyes. Researchers are also worried about the long-term effects of the drug on young children who use it. Some evidence suggests it could be responsible for changes in bone structure in patients who are still growing.

Perhaps the most disturbing part of the Accutane story began to emerge after it was approved for use for severe cystic acne in 1982. Some women who had taken the drug while pregnant lost their babies, and others gave birth to children with serious birth defects— missing ears, deformed faces, heart defects, or nerve damage. In some cases, the women became pregnant accidentally and continued to take the acne drug for a while before they realized they were pregnant. Even stopping Accutane treatments before starting a pregnancy may not help, because the drug remains in the bloodstream for a month or two after it is discontinued.

When these problems were reported, consumer groups campaigned against overprescribing Accutane. (Some enthusiastic doctors had been using the new "wonder drug" for mild forms of acne, when safer medications would be just as effective.) The Food and Drug Administration (FDA), which regulates all drugs sold in the United States, launched a public information campaign to warn women about the potential dangers of the new acne drug. Hoffmann–LaRoche, the drug's manufacturer, joined in the effort and strengthened its warnings to patients and doctors. In 1984 the FDA warned blood banks not to accept blood from donors who use or have used Accutane in the recent past. Doctors were also urged to require pregnancy tests for all female Accutane users.

Accutane was in the headlines again in 1988. Concerned about the fact that birth defects linked to the drug were still being reported, the FDA required Hoffmann–LaRoche to provide unprecedented labeling of the product, which would guarantee that its users realized the possible consequences. The drug is now sold in blister packages, with a warning on the wrapping of each individual capsule. A picture of a baby with birth defects is included, to call attention to the warning. In addition, Hoffmann-LaRoche will pay for birth-control counseling and a pregnancy test for any woman using Accutane.

Even with all these precautions, many consumer groups have tried to have the drug banned altogether. "We did consider withdrawing it," said an FDA spokesperson, "but we had to consider that 70 percent of the users of Accutane are either men or women who are not considered at risk of pregnancy. To deprive those individuals of access to a drug that provides a cure to a lifetime of scarring and disfigurement was more than we could bring ourselves to do."

DOING YOUR PART

Whatever form of treatment your doctor prescribes, you should follow it as faithfully as you can. Your condition will clear up only if you work hard at it. If anything out of the ordinary occurs—swelling, intense pain, or discomfort—always notify the doctor immediately. Except in the case of a reaction like this, however, you should not discontinue use of an acne medication on your own without the doctor telling you to do so. Suddenly stopping treatment could cause a severe flare-up.

ACNE SURGERY

In addition to prescriptions the doctor can recommend for you to take at home, he or she can perform procedures in the office to help alleviate acne problems.

Acne surgery includes a wide range of treatments. The simplest forms of acne surgery are when the doctor drains individual whiteheads or blackheads under sterile conditions. (Remember, even though you may be tempted to do this yourself, most doctors recommend that you shouldn't "pop" pimples, because you could do more damage and maybe even cause scarring.)

Some people go to skin-care salons to have blackheads and whiteheads removed, as well as to receive cleansing facial masks, which sometimes help speed up the acne process for faster-clearing skin. You should check with your doctor, and let him or her know exactly what other treatments you are receiving so that the doctor can take them into account in evaluating the results of treatments and prescribing new ones.

Acne surgery also includes much more serious procedures than just draining blackheads. Larger cysts are sometimes cut open, and the entire infected cyst is removed. Sometimes doctors will inject *steroids* (an anti-inflammatory cortisone drug, for example) into individual large pimples or cysts to reduce the swelling. But too much steroid medication can produce additional acnelike breakouts. Doctors also can apply a chemical that will peel away layers of skin. *Trichloroacetic acid* causes the skin to dry up and peel, which helps to open and drain acne pimples. Sometimes stronger peels are used. In severe acne cases doctors may use *carbon dioxide slush,* which causes the skin to peel by subjecting it to extremely low temperatures. Large cysts can also be removed by freezing them with liquid nitrogen. This is called *cryosurgery* (*cryo-* means "to freeze").

SCARRING

For some people, acne is more than just an embarrassing problem that they eventually outgrow. Sometimes permanent scars are left behind. Over time, some of them will become less noticeable, but many will remain long after acne pimples are gone. Dermatologists have ways to help people to reduce the amount of their acne scars and improve their complexions.

There are two types of acne scars. The most common are the *depressed scars,* sometimes called pockmarks or craters. The others are raised scars called *keloid scars,* which are commonly found in black people who get acne scars.

A doctor can tackle depressed acne scars in two ways. The most obvious method is to "plump up" the depression so that it is even with the rest of the skin. The other is to make the scar less visible by cutting down the edges around the depression.

The second method has been the most commonly used. *Dermabrasion* is the process by which the dermatologist planes down the skin around the scar to make it less noticeable. A high-speed diamond-tipped rotary brush is used like an electric sander. This may not sound too pleasant, and it is usually not a pleasant experience. A local anesthetic is used, and after the procedure an antibiotic lotion is applied and bandages are placed over the area. Scabs will form over the sanded areas, and when they fall off, new, smoother skin should be the result. However, it is usually quite a while—a week to a month or more—before the skin looks normal.

Some problems with dermabrasion are that the new skin is particularly sensitive to the sun, and it may tan differently from the rest of the face. In addition, the skin may become traumatized, and keloid scars may form. What's more, dermabrasion is by no means cheap. Even with all of its negative points, though, many people choose dermabrasion because they feel the long-term effects of a better-looking complexion are worth the risks and temporary pain and discomfort.

The same type of effect can be produced with chemicals rather than by physically sanding down the skin. *Chemabrasion,* or chemical peeling, is the application of a chemical, such as trichloroacetic acid, to the area. It burns the outer layers of skin and often feels quite painful. For several days the face will be swollen and red and will peel extensively. As soon as the skin is healed, a second treatment will be given. The peeling skin around the scar will make the pit look less deep and obvious. Sometimes the doctor will perform many smaller applications over a period of several months with a milder concentration of chemicals. Chemabrasion is not as effective as dermabrasion, but it is not as risky, and the recuperation time is much shorter. The same side effects present with dermabrasion also apply to chemabrasion.

The other method for removing scars is to work from below the surface. The depressions are raised by plumping them up. Not all doctors can perform these newer techniques, so if you are interested you should check with more than one doctor. One important method is the *fibrin foam method,* which was developed by Dr. Arthur Spangler. Fibrin is a natural body chemical found in blood. It forms the framework for blood clots. A doctor using the fibrin foam method takes some of your blood, and a laboratory then removes the fibrin protein, converting it into a foam that the doctor can inject into an individual scar. During each visit the doctor treats several scars at a time. The fibrin foam produces a slight inflammation under the skin, which causes scar tissue to form beneath the pit. After a few months, the scar will plump up enough so that it will not be as obvious.

The only drawback to this procedure, which is much less painful than dermabrasion, is that it is quite expensive. Collagen or gelatin may be used for the injections instead of fibrin foam. These newer techniques are still in somewhat experimental stages, and finding someone qualified to perform them may be difficult; but they certainly will be major methods of scar correction in the future.

Keloid scars are even more difficult to treat. These

raised scars can be planed down, but often the trauma to the skin causes new scars to form. Steroid injections can sometimes be used to shrink the scars. Another promising technique involves Cordran tape (manufactured by Lilly). This is a tape that is applied over the scar, flattening it down, while the cortisone in it acts to shrink the scar. After several applications, the scar eventually flattens down enough so that it is much less noticeable.

These are just some of the many ways a doctor can help with acne, and new methods of treatment are being developed. Others are only a short time away from being made available to all acne sufferers.

7

The Future in Acne Treatments

Acne treatments have come a long way over the years. In the not so distant past, doctors used to prescribe x-ray treatment for their acne patients. This was during a time when x-rays were used rather casually, even for trivial things like fitting shoes. People didn't realize the hazardous long-term effects that too much exposure to radiation such as x-rays could cause—cancer, for instance. This is one acne treatment doctors never use today.

Another popular treatment of the past was brown soap, which roughed away the skin. All this did was make the face extremely raw, and it was not very effective. It wasn't until benzoyl peroxide was discovered to be an effective acne treatment that other products such as sulfur, resorcinol, and salicylic acid became outdated.

Noticing that many women had acne flare-ups at the time of their menstrual period—when higher levels of progesterone are present—and that women taking birth control pills often were free from acne problems, doctors sometimes prescribed high-estrogen birth control pills for women with acne. However, this type of pill is no longer widely used, because some feel it might be linked with cancer in women.

Sunlamps were once commonly used in acne treatment. The drying and peeling effects of the sun helped speed up the acne process, and ultraviolet rays added a bacteria-killing effect that penetrated down into the pores. However, today this method is not as popular as it used to be, because over the years many people have suffered severe burns while taking sunlamp treatments on their own and because the damaging effects of ultraviolet light have become much better known.

When Accutane became available, everyone thought it was the wonder drug acne specialists had been waiting for; unfortunately, many unpleasant and dangerous side effects come along with this drug. However, with every new discovery, new avenues of research are opening up. Researchers have found that the active ingredient in Accutane, isotretinoin, is fairly effective when it is used in a gel form rather than in pill form. Although not as effective as Accutane, it is free of many of the side effects.

Over the years many "natural" remedies have been proclaimed as beneficial in clearing up acne. Zinc, vitamin B, vitamin E, yeast, and acidophilus (the bacteria in yogurt) have all been claimed as acne banishers at one time or another. Although no conclusive scientific evidence exists at the moment to support these claims, some researchers are exploring these avenues as well.

Another major breakthrough in acne treatment has been the combination approach. The most common combination therapy used is benzoyl peroxide with antibiotics (both oral and topical). The benzoyl peroxide loosens the outer layer of skin, allowing the bacteria-killing antibiotic to penetrate into the follicles better. Benzoyl peroxide and Retin-A make another effective combination for fighting comedones. Researchers are also combining other commonly used treatments and finding that the combined effect is much better than that of either drug used separately.

One interesting acne treatment discovered by researchers at the University of Michigan is a combination of the antibiotic tetracycline with the pain reliever ibuprofen (found in Advil and Nuprin). Patients in the study who had moderate to severe acne showed definite improvement. Like aspirin, ibuprofen not only relieves pain but also reduces swelling, which is probably the reason for its effectiveness against acne lesions.

In another study, patients with severe cystic acne were treated with a combination of a synthetic form of a vitamin A derivative and a steroid drug called dexamethasone, which is chemically related to cortisone. After a six-month treatment with the combination, most of the patients showed remarkable progress.

These studies are all quite promising, and many different choices are available to your doctor. Remember never to mix acne products on your own, however, because only the doctor knows which ones are safe to mix. Some, when combined, will cause the skin to dry out too much and can cause serious problems and discomfort.

Sometimes acne research results in breakthroughs that can help people with other kinds of problems as well. A discovery concerning Retin-A made headlines all around the world in 1988. Researchers found that this acne comedone fighter is also effective in reducing wrinkles in skin. One reason aging skin looks older is that new epidermal cells are not produced as often as in younger skin. Retin-A increases the turnover rate of the epidermal cells, and it also increases the blood flow to the area. The result can be smoother, softer, younger-looking skin with a healthy, rosy glow.

Drugstores all around the country were suddenly running out of the drug as people worried about wrinkles asked their doctors for Retin-A prescriptions. Many people, expecting a wonder drug, were disappointed. Retin-A takes many months before any real results can be seen, and often the skin looks worse before it gets better. Not too many people were willing to stick it out long enough to get their younger-looking skin.

Finding a cure for acne may not rank as high as finding a cure for cancer, heart disease, or AIDS, but it could save millions of people a lot of misery. One study found that patients with severe acne often had very low self-esteem. After successfully undergoing treatment and clearing up their acne, they had a much better opinion of themselves. They were no longer plagued by the anxiety and depression that had been draining their energy and blighting their lives.

Today many more treatments are available to acne sufferers than in the past, and most cases of acne are treatable. Researchers all over the world are working hard to find a real cure for this bothersome condition that affects almost all of us. When they succeed at last, adolescence will be a little easier, and teens will have one less problem to face.

Glossary

acne a skin disorder in which the follicles of the oil glands become blocked and inflamed, producing pimples or cysts.

acnegenic producing acne.

androgen male sex hormone.

antibiotic a drug that kills bacteria.

astringent a substance used to tighten the skin and remove oil from it.

basal layer a layer of living cells at the bottom of the epidermis from which new epidermal cells are formed.

chemabrasion chemical treatment to peel down the skin around a depressed scar.

closed comedo a "whitehead"; a comedo that is almost completely plugged.

collagen a fibrous, elastic protein found in skin and other tissues.

comedo (pl. **comedones**) a stopped-up follicle.

comedogenic producing comedones.

cyst an infection enclosed in a capsulelike membrane below the skin surface.

depressed scar a scar that is lower than the surface of the surrounding skin; a pockmark, pit, or crater.

dermabrasion planing down the skin around a depressed scar to make the scar less noticeable.

dermis the layer making up about 90 percent of the skin. It is composed of living cells and collagen fibers; contains nerve endings, blood vessels, sweat glands, oil glands, and hair follicles; and is covered by the epidermis.

epidermis the covering layer of the skin, the outermost cells of which are dead and form a horny, protective coating.

exfoliant a substance that causes the skin to peel.

follicle a tubelike structure opening to the surface; especially the hair follicle from which a hair grows and into which oil glands empty.

keloid scar a raised scar formed by overgrowth of skin cells during healing of a lesion.

keratin a horny protein found in epidermal cells, hair, and nails.

lesion an injury or abnormal change in the body; acne lesions (pimples) range in severity from microcomedones through closed comedones, open comedones, papules, pustules, and nodules, to cysts.

microcomedo a microscopic comedo.

microflora bacteria and other microorganisms that normally live in or on the body.

nodule a large papule with substantial inflammation in the dermis.

open comedo a "blackhead"; a comedo in which the pore is open and the sebum plug is visible at the surface.

papule a ruptured follicle at an early stage of inflammation.

pimple a papule or pustule.

pore a tiny opening, for example, from a sweat gland or a hair follicle.

pustule a ruptured follicle with a pus-filled sac.

sebaceous gland oil gland.

sebum the oily secretion of the sebaceous gland.

subcutaneous layer the layer of supporting tissue beneath the dermis.

topical medication a drug that is applied to the skin rather than taken internally.

Index